garden
boundaries

garden
boundaries

USING WALLS, FENCEWORK AND HEDGES TO DEFINE YOUR GARDEN

JENNY HENDY

LORENZ BOOKS

This edition is published by Lorenz Books

Lorenz Books is an imprint of
Anness Publishing Limited
Hermes House, 88–89 Blackfriars Road,
London SE1 8HA
tel. 020 7401 2077; fax 020 7633 9499
www.lorenzbooks.com; info@anness.com

© Anness Publishing Ltd 2004

UK agent: The Manning Partnership Ltd,
6 The Old Dairy Melcombe Road, Bath BA2 3LR;
tel. 01225 478 444; fax 01225 478 440;
sales@manning-partnership.co.uk

UK distributor: Grantham Book Services Ltd,
Isaac Newton Way, Alma Park Industrial Estate, Grantham,
Lincs NG31 9SD; tel. 01476 541080; fax 01476 541061;
orders@gbs.tbs-ltd.co.uk

North American agent/distributor: National Book
Network, 4501 Forbes Boulevard, Suite 200, Lanham,
MD 20706; tel. 301 459 3366; fax 301 429 5746;
www.nbnbooks.com

Australian agent/distributor: Pan Macmillan Australia,
Level 18 St Martins Tower, 31 Market St, Sydney,
NSW 2000; tel. 1300 135 113; fax 1300 135 103;
customer.service@macmillan.com.au

A CIP catalogue record for this book is available from
the British Library.

Publisher: *Joanna Lorenz*
Editorial Director: *Helen Sudell*
Senior Editor: *Sarah Ainley*
Designer: *Louise Clements*
Indexer: *Helen Snaith*
Production Controller: *Stephen Lang*

1 2 3 4 5 6 7 8 9 10

contents

introduction

Human beings are territorial animals and we feel most relaxed when our private space is clearly defined. In some gardens the area feels too open to be intimate, and no one likes to sit with their back exposed, especially to passers-by and prying eyes.

The natural inclination is to separate off the outside world and erect screens and divides that create garden "rooms" of the right scale and proportion, so that we can escape to a tranquil haven. The design and decorative finishing of a wide variety of boundaries is the subject of this book.

When you first enter a garden, especially one with no internal divisions, the eye races to the margins, calculating the size of the plot. Unless there is a strong focus within the garden, it will be the walls, fences and hedges that attract the eye, leaving no doubt as to the extent of the site. If you want to create the illusion of space in a rural garden, you can establish boundaries that are virtually invisible, blending into the surrounding landscape. In urban locations, bold architectural lines, colours and decorative detailing can define or support the style or character of the garden.

This book brings together a collection of boundary ideas to suit any theme, from contemporary to period and urban to rustic. Whether you wish to create new external boundaries, or strengthen or upgrade existing ones, this beautifully illustrated book offers a wealth of practical advice and innovative ideas to get you started.

ABOVE: *A window framed with climbers perforates this stone wall, letting in light and allowing glimpses of the garden beyond.*

RIGHT: *This contemporary version of a Chinese moon gate makes a delightful entrance to a children's play garden.*

One of the first things people do when they move into a new property is erect a barrier to define their space and create a sense of privacy.

Boundaries should not be thought of as purely functional. We might need them to keep children safely in the garden or to shelter plants from the prevailing wind, but there is also tremendous scope for making walls, screens, gateways and hedges an integral part of the garden layout and styling.

Of course, there are budget considerations, but imaginatively designed, well-built boundaries help to form the bones of the garden and can make a pleasing backdrop long before the plants start to mature.

It is always interesting to see materials mixed in an unusual way, such as hazel hurdles with galvanized posts or rough stone pillars with rendered panels. Varying the height of structures or incorporating innovative touches, such as windows, arched doorways, niches and seating bays, can quickly turn barriers into wonderful garden features.

boundary design

fences

When boundaries need to be established instantly and relatively inexpensively, fencing is one of the best options, providing privacy and shelter but taking up next to no space.

TOP: *This innovative fencing is made from spaced timber uprights, which ensure security but at the same time create an airy feel.*

ABOVE: *Normally associated with rustic style, hazel hurdles set into a timber framework create an effective backdrop for this smart roof terrace.*

Most mass-produced wooden fencing panels are made from treated softwood planks that are woven or overlapped and held in a rigid frame. They are available in a range of heights depending on how much of a barrier you require, and shorter panels allow you the option of combining them with more decorative trellis sections. Softened with climbing plants and wall shrubs, or coated with coloured paints and stains, fence panels can be made to fit in with most styles of house and garden. Just bear in mind that fences do have quite a "suburban" look, and might seem out of place in situations such as the formal grounds of larger period properties.

For old-fashioned cottage gardens, the traditional picket fence would be perfectly in keeping. Hazel hurdles, attached to metal angle irons, can also be used as a backdrop to rustic country-style gardens, but they can work well in more modern environments too – for example, screening a smart city terrace or roof garden. In this kind of setting you might frame the hurdles with stout sawn timbers or set them between aluminium fence posts. Hurdles can be expected to last for only around eight years before they start to disintegrate, but they are easy to replace.

Standard fencing panels are attached to wooden fencing posts that have been tanalized to slow down rotting. To make the inevitable replacement of the posts an easier proposition, and to help keep the base of the post relatively dry, instead of setting them into concrete fix them into metal sockets. These are attached to a long spike that can either be driven into the ground, using a special tool, or set in concrete. An even more foolproof method, though not the most attractive option, is to slot the panels into grooves in concrete posts. With the addition of concrete base sections to keep the wood from making contact with the damp earth, there is very little chance of the panels rotting, and replacement is straightforward.

RIGHT: *A topping of trellis panels gives climbers, such as roses, clematis and honeysuckle, something to attach themselves to and helps soften the appearance of solid fencing.*

BELOW: *Picket fencing is an archetypal boundary material for country cottages but here it is used to give a feminine touch to the garden of a town house. Notice how it picks up on the delicate fretwork and trellis panelling around the doorway. This type of fencing is quite easy to assemble from component parts and is best suited to small-scale areas.*

screens

Walls and fences form a solid divide, but sometimes you need to take a more subtle approach, especially when you are working within the boundaries of a small plot. This is where screens are very useful.

Perforated screens provide tantalizing glimpses of the garden or the world outside, while still acting as an effective physical barrier. Even if you are lucky enough to look out on to wonderful views of the sea or mountains you will probably still feel the need to have some protection from the wind and prying eyes, especially when sitting and relaxing in the garden. Screens can be used to outline a space that has a particular function, such as an outdoor dining room or children's play area, while allowing the planting on the other side to show through. This arrangement lets in plenty of light and prevents small spaces from feeling claustrophobic. A screen can be either straight or curving – perhaps following the sinuous line of a pathway – and can help to guide foot traffic, preventing people from taking shortcuts across the grass.

Trellis panels are ideal for straightforward rectilinear screening, but curved panels allow you to be more flexible in your design, introducing meandering lines and making elegant circular shelters to surround seating areas. However, trellis does tend to add a particular style that may be at odds with a relaxed rural garden or ultra-modern plot. Here you can afford to be a little more adventurous in the choice of materials and design, using heavy wooden posts or metal scaffolding poles to make curving screens. Reclaimed timber planks can be set in the ground, end-on at an angle, so that the view through them changes as you pass and is at some point completely closed off.

OPPOSITE: *To create a sense of seclusion in a raised outdoor dining area without blocking out the light, the owners have erected a partial screen of horizontal wooden planks. To provide midday shade, a bamboo blind can be rolled down.*

RIGHT: *Painted wooden posts or metal rods can be set in the ground at different heights to form undulating curves. This is a totally flexible system, which is ideal for making partitions within an informal garden.*

LEFT: *Acting almost like a piece of artwork, this trellis panel appears to cut through the hedge at right angles. From a practical and aesthetic standpoint, creating a foreground planting for square or diamond lattice trelliswork is an excellent solution for screening off utility areas or for separating parts of the garden that have a different character or purpose.*

OPPOSITE ABOVE: *Sometimes it is worth thinking outside the box and looking further than the off-the-peg range of screening and fencing materials. Here, for example, bamboo canes – quite possibly reused beanpoles – have been used to divide a vegetable plot. The canes are attached to wires strained between wooden posts and can be set as wide or as close as desired, ready to support annual climbers such as sweet peas.*

OPPOSITE BELOW: *Certain types of custom-built screening, such as this bamboo lattice panel, can be used as highly decorative inserts within a boundary or as stand-alone features. Panels of decorative trelliswork, known as treillage, would work well in a classically inspired garden and you can also make your own designs using tanalized roofing laths. For radiating "spokes" wooden dowelling is ideal.*

For continuous screens or perforated panels within solid barriers there are other materials to consider, depending on the style of the garden. For example, you could use willow wands to weave a design across a gap in the hedge. To make "walls" in a pergola walkway that forms a boundary or an internal division of the garden, you could go for a hi-tech option and use sheets of wire gauze or galvanized mesh grille. The former can be illuminated at night using coloured lights shining up from the base – the effect is surprisingly delicate. The latter makes an excellent climbing frame for plants with tendrils, and would soon be softened by leafy growth.

One of the simplest forms of screening for urban plots involves a framework of fence posts joined by cross-bars top and bottom; fencing planks are attached, but instead of butting them up against one another, you leave even gaps to give a filtered view. Screens made from bark-covered poles suit wild gardens and country-style plots to a tee. The designs are usually very simple, such as a criss-cross or diamond pattern, and are not difficult to construct provided you have pre-cut notches so that you can fix the rounded sections together easily.

In naturalistic gardens with an Oriental influence, modern fencing and trellis could look out of place, but there are products available from garden centres and do-it-yourself stores that would blend in nicely. For example, dark heather screens are rustic and unobtrusive, especially when the posts are stained the same colour. Pale-coloured split bamboo screens are more eye-catching and create a distinctly Oriental atmosphere. Neither material allows you to see through, but light does penetrate. You can also buy rolls of these materials, which, as they are thin and flexible, can easily be attached to a wooden frame of your own design, using a staple gun. To make a more transparent screen you could create a framework and then attach willow wands or bamboo canes at intervals, spacing them according to the amount of privacy you require.

For a really authentic feel, use traditional Japanese lashed bamboo screens and panels. These are still produced following centuries-old designs, all with different names. You can hire specialist companies to advise on and build such screens on site, but they are also available direct from Japan via the internet.

trellis

Fences made from trellis panels let more light into an area and, though they are perforated, the network of wooden slats baffles the eye and tends to keep your attention forward of the boundary.

The style and quality of ready-made trellis panels varies tremendously and it is well worth shopping around. Disregard flimsy panels – they won't last long and will soon start to look shabby. When using trellis alone for boundaries, always use heavy fencing posts, at least 10cm (4in) square: don't be tempted to save money by using smaller supports. The structure will appear insubstantial and out of scale with the architecture of the house and garden.

To retain a light and airy feel in the garden, while at the same time maintaining privacy, you can either use trellis panels with foreground planting to the required height – such as a mixed border with plenty of evergreens – or make the bottom two-thirds of the fence from solid panels. If you take the second option, remember that the fencing posts need to be tall enough to accommodate both panels and trellis.

For small quantities of trellis, it is possible to make your own simple rectangular panels using tanalized roofing laths (available from builders' merchants and do-it-yourself stores), nailed together or stapled with an industrial-quality staple gun. Although it is a time-consuming process, home-construction allows you to make panels to your own design. For example, trellis "mesh" is often quite small, but for a modern, minimalist garden you might find that simplified panels with larger

ABOVE LEFT: *Trellis panels look best when fixed between very sturdy posts, which give an impression of rigidity and structure.*

LEFT: *This balcony garden has a room-like atmosphere, thanks to the trelliswork that runs along the top of the low wall.*

OPPOSITE: *Different styles of trellis suit certain design themes, and here the curved panels and diamond latticework fit in beautifully with this Spanish colonial-style pool garden. In addition to its practical function, trellis like this can add an extra dimension of pattern and texture to a garden.*

squares work better. If you are looking for something more decorative, in either a square or diamond pattern, perhaps incorporating curves, you will find that the off-the-peg choice, even from garden centres, is now very large. More highly designed, less functional panels are known as treillage and these are ideal for use in period-style gardens. Quality ready-made or custom-built treillage can be very expensive but may be a good investment for long-term constructions, especially if the materials used are 100 per cent tanalized.

One of the advantages of using fencing and trellis panels set at regular intervals is that it sets up a pleasing visual rhythm: the fence posts provide the regular beat and the curving trellis sections sweep the eye from one point to the next. You can strengthen the repeated vertical elements by attaching finials to the tops of the posts. This type of well-defined boundary works well in gardens with a formal layout, where line and pattern are so important, but also helps to support billowing, romantic borders by introducing an element of structure.

walls

Although boundaries made from bricks and mortar or stone are often the most expensive options, they can be highly effective in terms of the overall design of the garden.

Well-constructed walls create an atmosphere of stability and maturity within the garden. Though relatively costly, they are a long-term investment and can add significantly to the value of the property. However, the materials used for building walls are critical to the success of the construction. Front garden boundaries, in particular, should reflect the surrounding architectural styles and vernacular materials in order to blend in seamlessly. For example, a red brick wall would stand out awkwardly in a place where the local rough-quarried stone was the principle building material.

You can mix and match design elements to draw contrasting themes together, perhaps linking modern and traditional, but it is important to retain some kind of visual link, however subtle, either with the house itself or with the walls and buildings in the immediate vicinity. To take one example, if you were enclosing a garden attached to a brick-built house located in an area of the country where the buildings were faced with flint nodules, you could insert panels of flint into the wall facing the road. This would ground the house and garden, and make them feel part of the landscape.

Sourcing walling materials that match or blend with the house can be time-consuming and you may have to look in architectural salvage yards for reclaimed bricks or dressed stone blocks, particularly for period properties. If you are employing builders, ask them to provide samples of the materials to be used before work begins. Even if you can manage only a close approximation, sometimes the addition of original coping stones can tie everything together nicely – you might, for instance, use clay pantiles, slates or tiles that match the house roof for this purpose. An alternative solution, if authentic materials are limited, would be to build an inexpensive wall from rendered breezeblocks (cinderblocks) that features just a few bricks or stones showing through the rendering.

OPPOSITE: *When a wall has as much character as this it is important to strike a balance between the parts that are covered with plants and those left bare. Rather than using trellis, opt for "invisible" wires to support the plants.*

ABOVE: *This skilfully constructed slate wall makes a feature at the back of a vegetable garden, where its somewhat rustic appearance fits in perfectly. Some holes were deliberately left for planting to mimic natural colonization by seedlings.*

Traditional dry-stone walls work well in a relaxed country- or cottage-garden setting, particularly if you live in an area where walls are used to surround farmland. Because they are constructed without mortar, you can plant directly into the sides. Though rough-quarried stone is normally used, slate offers more opportunities for incorporating decorative effects. It is easily split to produce thin, flat pieces that craftsmen are able to arrange in a variety of patterns. Beautifully textured walls of this kind are reminiscent of those seen in Arts and Crafts gardens. However, this type of walling has a highly dynamic quality that would also allow it to work well in modern, minimalist urban settings.

It is well worth planning the design of a new wall carefully before construction, because there are all kinds of devices that could enhance its appearance, adding to the garden as a whole. For example, you could incorporate a bay to accommodate a bench seat, or a niche or alcove to display a bust, sculpture or vase. You might even decide to do away with straight lines altogether and build a serpentine wall for an air of eccentricity or perhaps one with a gentle curving profile. Bear in mind that walls don't have to be the same height all the way along their length: in some situations it might be appropriate for a wall to taper seamlessly down to almost ground level or dip occasionally to provide a view of the landscape beyond.

Although the wall may require only minimal supporting elements, you could enhance the design by emphasizing these, perhaps including taller pillars or substantial buttresses to set up a visual rhythm. This would be expensive in brick or stone, but the much cheaper breezeblock (cinderblock) is easy to manipulate; once rendered and painted, it can be very hard to tell the difference. Finishing touches can be instrumental in developing the character of a rendered construction. For example, whitewashed walls with a coping of terracotta tiles would immediately suggest hot Mediterranean climes.

ABOVE: *Slate is a wonderful material for dry-stone walling; when it is cut and laid to give a smooth façade, the results can look surprisingly contemporary. The rugged texture makes an interesting foil for airy plants.*

OPPOSITE TOP: *The sculptural nature of this curving wall enhances the look of this heathland garden.*

OPPOSITE BELOW: *This rammed earth wall adds a novelty feature to the garden.*

Substantial boundary walls evoke an atmosphere of timelessness, turning the garden into a protected haven.

For a substantial wall, perhaps with a curving profile, the least expensive option may be reinforced concrete poured on site using a mould of wooden shuttering. Needless to say, this is a job for the professionals. Concrete is extremely versatile in terms of the shapes that can be created, but also because it can be pigmented before pouring to achieve dramatic and avant-garde effects, such as bands of colour. Subtlety is also possible, and you could mimic a traditional Oriental rammed earth wall using random layers of differently toned batches.

hedges

By far the cheapest way to create a visually solid boundary is to plant a hedge. Formal clipped hedges, whether they are evergreen or deciduous, can be very effective substitutes for bricks and mortar.

TOP: *Hedges can be decorative in their own right, with attractive flowers or, as in this case, alternating light and dark green Leyland cypress (x* Cupressocyparis leylandii*) with a stepped profile to highlight the change in colour.*

ABOVE: *Formal hedging provides a backdrop for colourful garden planting and decorative structures.*

OPPOSITE: *Low box hedging marks out the formal ground plan of this classically inspired garden.*

Using hedging as a type of living architecture has its downsides, as it will need a few years to become established and will require continued maintenance. That said, there is almost no limit to the shapes and effects you can create with regular clipping, and, on a more creative level, hedge-cutting is considered by many to be a branch of the art of topiary.

Some of the classic hedge plants have the ability to regenerate from old, bare wood if cut hard back. This makes them much easier to keep to a particular size or shape. Yew (*Taxus baccata*), holly (*Ilex aquifolium*) and box (*Buxus sempervirens*), all of which thrive in light shade, are evergreen. Privet (*Ligustrum ovalifolium*) and pyracantha are semi-evergreen, while beech (*Fagus sylvatica*) and hornbeam (*Carpinus betulus*) both hang on to their coppery autumn foliage until the new growth replaces it in the spring. These last two are often used for larger boundary walls and structures, such as stilt hedges, for which the branches are cleared from the base to leave a clean stem and the top is trained horizontally by tying the branches on to a framework of canes.

Fast-growing conifers are a popular choice for hedges and include the notorious Leyland cypress (x *Cupressocyparis leylandii*) and the more easily controlled *Thuja plicata*. Both can be trained successfully but need frequent attention to prevent them getting out of hand as neither regenerates when cut back to old bare branches. Leylandii can be kept to only 30cm (12in) wide and 2m (6ft 6in) high if it is trained from the beginning, and its speed of growth makes it useful for creating features such as colonnades: simply trim the base of the plants to form a pillar and allow the tops to grow out to meet at the top and form an arch. In an ordinary hedge, you will sometimes see a gold-leaf cultivar mixed in to create a regular rhythm, perhaps with one type being clipped as pillars to accentuate the difference even further.

There are two profiles to a formal hedge. In one, the sides and top are perfectly straight, which is suitable when the hedge has plenty of light. The other is to clip the hedge wider at the bottom. The advantage here is that light falls evenly on the foliage, preventing the bottom from becoming threadbare.

The top and sides can be further sculpted and may include buttressing or pillars topped with clipped finials. Sometimes the top is scalloped or castellated, or cut into stylized birds and animals. Curving shapes can be difficult to construct in brick or stone, but with forward planning you can create alcoves or semicircular bays in a hedge, known as exedras. One unusual technique that is seen with established yew and box hedging is to clip following the natural growth of the plant. The hedge develops billowing contours and lots of character. Avant-garde shaping works well in the vicinity of modern architecture, such as sweeping, wavelike curves or a serpentine profile.

One of the most appealing aspects of formal hedging is the contrast between its perfectly sculpted form and the haphazard jumble of foliage and flowers that surrounds it. In rural areas, clipped hedges also make an intriguing boundary between the garden proper and the wild landscape beyond. Here, the hedge marks the limit of human control over nature.

ABOVE LEFT: *Dark hedging fronted by pale catmint makes a striking feature.*

ABOVE: *The architectural leaves of cardoons in this ornamental vegetable plot appear even more dramatic against the backdrop of a close-clipped hedge.*

OPPOSITE: *A beautiful rose hedge billows out over rustic fencing.*

Hedges and living screens made from flowering shrubs and foliage plants can be much less structured. You may need to allow room for the branches to spread naturally, since giving plants a severe haircut mid-season can spoil their appearance. Informal hedges may not provide as much security as those with a dense, clipped structure. *Rosa rugosa* is a good choice for a flowering hedge. It has fragrant blooms, healthy foliage, colourful hips in autumn that birds love to eat, and thorny stems. In an Oriental-style garden you might plant bamboo such as *Phyllostachys aurea* or *Fargesia murielae*. On the coast, try hedges of mop-head hydrangeas (*Hydrangea macrophylla*), pink-flowered tamarisk or silver-grey-leaved sea buckthorn (*Hippophae rhamnoides*). In an exposed rural location, a mixed hedge of native species would form an effective barrier to livestock, as well as providing food and habitat for wildlife.

Formal hedges can be thought of as green architecture, adding a pleasing sense of structure to the garden.

railings

Cast or wrought ironwork tends to be associated with period properties and the front gardens of smart town houses, but today's designers have brought about something of a renaissance in metal.

Though formal railings still have their place, especially when topping brick or stone walling, blacksmiths are now being commissioned to produce more abstract creations that take advantage of the malleability of metal. While still functioning as boundaries, some metal screens and panels act almost as works of art in their own right in the garden. In modern and rural settings alike, abstract metalwork may be left untreated so that it rusts, producing a textured surface and developing beautiful shades of red, brown and orange.

In the hands of a skilled craftsman, iron can be wrought into delicate designs, perhaps featuring leaves, tendrils and blooms. Inspiration from nature may also lead to less obvious designs, such as spiders' webs or more avant-garde elements including water ripples. You may be able to find decorative panels like this in architectural salvage yards but you could also commission railings, metal screens and gates to your own design or to fit in with surrounding properties.

Railings can be plain or quite elaborate, with barley twist stems and other decorative flourishes, including finials. Traditional spikes and arrowheads are undoubtedly useful as a deterrent to burglars, but they also produce an elegant finish. Sometimes railings have a bowed profile or the tops are curled over to give a softer look. Cast iron panels are not as easy to come by, but are also worth searching out, many being attractively embellished. Formal railings contrast beautifully with surrounding planting and architecture when coated with high-gloss paint. It can be effective to pick out some minor design details of wrought or cast iron panels using a contrasting shade or, for a touch of luxury, gold leaf.

Country-style or farm railings are simple and functional: a good choice for rural gardens, where you want to keep out livestock but at the same time give the impression that the plot blends into the surrounding countryside.

OPPOSITE: *The elegant designs of antique wrought iron panels are perfect for period gardens. Seek out originals at architectural salvage yards or commission reproductions or original contemporary pieces from blacksmiths. The fluid style of some modern creations works particularly well in rusting mild steel.*

ABOVE: *Set within a rigid framework and attached to brick pillars, this very simple design is functional but at the same time pleasing to the eye. This type of enclosure would be ideal around a raised deck or terraced sitting area for ensuring safety without jeopardizing the view.*

natural barriers

In rural gardens and properties on the edge of town that back on to open countryside, it can be a mistake to put up solid barriers, such as walls and fences, that will block a beautiful view.

The ideal solution for a garden facing on to scenic countryside might be to have completely open boundaries to preserve the view, but this is not always practical: sometimes sites are just too exposed to the elements. If you want the garden to merge softly into the wild planting beyond, one approach is to plant a shelter belt, using a mix of native and introduced tree species underplanted with shrubs.

When close-planted in copse formations, trees such as rowan, silver birch, pine and, for wet ground, alder can make an effective screen in just three or four years. Interplant deciduous species with evergreens, such as laurel and holly. Also, try mixing native woodland and hedgerow plants, such as hazel, field maple and blackthorn with more subdued garden varieties, such as weigela, white-flowered spiraea, coloured-stemmed dogwoods, large cotoneasters and shrub roses. This ensures a naturalistic feel and also provides cover and food for a variety of wildlife. As well as providing wind protection, this arrangement is also the best way to reduce noise pollution from a busy motorway or railway line. Try letting the grass in front of the trees grow long and cut the lawn to create a broad meandering margin of long grass. You could also cut a path that disappears through the trees.

Allowing gaps in the shelter belt, or border planting, is a technique called "borrowed landscape". In Japan, where it first developed, this landscaping art is known as *shakkei*.

OPPOSITE: *Areas of the garden where privacy is important, such as swimming pools, hot tubs and patios, can all be easily camouflaged by enclosing them with screens of loose-branched foliage plants, such as bamboo or sea buckthorn.*

ABOVE RIGHT: *Native trees planted with shrubs protect exposed gardens.*

RIGHT: *Staggered planting camouflages the garden boundary, leading the eye beyond the back row to make the garden feel bigger.*

It has the effect of incorporating the scenery beyond into the garden to make it appear bigger than it really is. The natural contouring of the land, combined with overlapping bands of planting, is used to blur the true boundary of the garden.

Another device for creating an invisible boundary between a cultivated garden and the surrounding fields is the ha-ha, a type of walled ditch championed by Capability Brown and exponents of the 18th-century Landscape Movement in Britain. Where the budget is limited, however, a simple fence may have to suffice, keeping out livestock as well as providing extra security. From a distance, certain types of fencing can be very unobtrusive. Farmers' barbed wire is not the safest material, especially if young children use the garden, but it is relatively inconspicuous. An easier material to use domestically is galvanized pig-wire fencing. This has a large square mesh design and can be attached to stout tanalized wooden posts. Another option is to thread galvanized fencing wire through black metal angle irons. Wooden ranch-style fencing is more obvious but still works well in a rural setting, especially if the wood is left to weather naturally.

To preserve elements of the view beyond the garden, you can leave gaps in the planting along the boundary, or use lower growing species in places. Another approach is to frame the view using staggered shrubs and trees, rather like stage scenery. Strategically placed planting allows you to screen out features such as roads, commercial buildings and electricity pylons.

Certain sections of the garden, including patios and eating areas, swimming pools and hot tubs, may need more intensive protection from wind and, for psychological reasons, a greater sense of seclusion. Here, an informal hedge or screen or a deep mixed border would enable inhabitants to relax more easily. Once wind protection has been established, you could add lush or exotic planting to give the area a unique character. Black windbreak mesh is unobtrusive, and when applied to the back of trellis panels it provides instant shelter for planting.

RIGHT: *Even when a garden is next to open fields, a deep backdrop of sheltering plants can create an oasis effect, allowing for more tender or large-leaved subjects to be grown.*

subtle boundaries

Solid boundaries, such as walls and fences, will often be inappropriate for a house on the beach or in a woodland clearing, that is surrounded by natural beauty. Here, a more unobtrusive approach is needed.

Wherever you live, from the heart of a wood to the middle of a modern housing estate, it is only natural to want to establish your territory, even if this is done in a subtle way. On a typical open-plan development, where planning restrictions don't allow conventional divisions in the form of fences or hedges, you can usually get away with planting a cluster of trees and shrubs, or an informal mixed border, to screen you from your neighbours, provided the planting doesn't interfere with the service strips. Think about planting in curving swathes, rather than narrow tramline borders, which don't allow for much in the way of imaginative planting. For example, in a contemporary-style front garden you could mix bold architectural evergreens, such as *Phormium tenax*, *Fatsia japonica* and *Juniperus* 'Sky Rocket', with grasses and sedges to complement the strong lines of the buildings and to make a real feature of the main doorway.

Meanwhile, low plantings may be augmented with coloured poles simply pushed into the ground, or you could try painted metal obelisks or topiary cones for a structured feel. To create a rhythm, use heavy rope swags fixed to short wooden posts (you can buy rope from ships' chandlers). Another low-level solution would be to use lights, perhaps solar-powered if it is difficult to get electricity out to them, set at intervals along the boundary. Ground-level uplighters can be angled to illuminate foliage from the base.

Smooth, rounded boulders, cobbles and pebbles make a wonderful foil for plants with grassy or sword-shaped leaves, and these days large rock monoliths are increasingly being used to add emphasis to informal boundaries, especially at key points, such as the mouth of a driveway. If you go for this option, make sure that when the quarry delivers, they lower the rock directly into its prepared socket, as you will never be able to move it yourself.

OPPOSITE ABOVE: *Here a clutch of large smooth cobbles helps to define an almost invisible boundary. On a larger scale, boulders or tall upright pieces of quarried stone can be used to mark entranceways.*

OPPOSITE BELOW: *An arc of tanalized logs set into concrete at different heights resembles a set of organ pipes. This type of boundary is ideal for separating planted areas from those surfaced with loose aggregates such as gravel.*

RIGHT: *Without spoiling the planting effect, a meandering line of painted rods weaves its way through. This would be an attractive solution for a shared front garden of open-plan design with broad swathes of foliage and flower.*

Around a shoreline property you might use reclaimed sleepers to create a low wall that varies in height. For an even more informal option, try using pieces of driftwood set end-on into the ground, or fishing creels piled with an assortment of pebbles and seashells collected from shoreline walks. Such low-key markers could be strengthened with groupings of salt- and wind-resistant plants, such as tamarisk, sea buckthorn (*Hippophae rhamnoides*), pines and dune grasses, avoiding planting in rows or straight lines, in order to maintain the relaxed seashore effect.

Stone cairns might work well to define a garden boundary at points along the margins of a rugged mountain or moorland garden, perhaps in association with a drainage ditch crossed by rough timber bridges – all of which give the impression of a mountain footpath, and help to link the garden to its surroundings.

On land belonging to a period property in the country, a more formal solution is likely to be required. You might choose traditional elements, such as a line of weathered staddlestones, or perhaps some classic topiary features. Lollipop-headed standards, trained from plants such as holly or *Prunus lusitanica,* would withstand the elements well and allow room for planting at the base, but you could also use clipped domes of box or yew set at regular intervals along the margins of the property. This would establish the garden boundary line, marking the limits of cultivation, in a style that fits with the character of the property, without disturbing the view of the open countryside beyond.

OPPOSITE: *Designs for canvas awnings and screens can be quite sculptural in effect. Here, a sweep of waterproof fabric provides privacy for the garden without cutting out any of the light. An added bonus is that the awning can be dismantled and packed away when not in use or during bad weather.*

TOP RIGHT: *Heavy rope swags attached to short wooden posts work well alongside wooden decking or an informal boardwalk.*

RIGHT: *For a seashore feel, combine beach shingle, pebbles and pieces of driftwood with wooden posts to make an informal garden boundary.*

entrances & gateways

When you step through a garden door or walk beneath an archway laden with climbing plants, you have an expectation that you are entering a place with a unique character, mood or atmosphere.

There are countless variations in the style and purpose of entrances. In a practical sense, they are simply gaps in the boundary that allow access to the garden. Yet they also signify a transition from one environment to another. You might step across the boundary from a busy street into a tranquil green haven, go from a formal garden with topiary and hedging to a wild meadow, or enter a surreal fantasy landscape via a conventional unassuming forecourt. Being able to see only glimpses of the area beyond adds to the feeling of suspense.

The style of the entrance can provide clues or visual signals about the owners of the property, as well as the nature of their garden: the grand gateways of old mansion houses clearly established the status of the residents. In rural settings it can be fun to reconstruct ostentatious gateposts topped with carved finials, or to acquire a set of ornate gates from an architectural salvage yard and use them to give an impression of faded elegance and the presence of an old estate.

Entrances can be augmented to give them greater prominence, and also to make the visitor feel more welcome. Low gates, in particular, benefit from being strengthened visually. Sometimes all that is needed is a simple metal hoop to form an archway, perhaps hung with a windchime or a lantern light. A more substantial timber and trellis archway would allow for decoration with flowering climbers. Hedging can be grown up around a framework to meet at the top or cut to create green pillars or curved "wings" on either side of the gate, and you could even clip ball–shaped finials.

In rural settings, simple wooden gates or ironwork are generally in keeping. Because of their organic flowing form, woven willow structures and rustic archways are ideal for entranceways bordering on to woodland or open fields. A heavy piece of reclaimed timber could be used to create a lintel for a doorway in a stone or rendered wall.

Opposite: *The overhead lamp above this arched, wrought iron gateway makes a feature of the entrance, giving a real welcome for visitors, especially when illuminated at nighttime.*

Top: *This wicker fence and arched entranceway feel perfectly in keeping with their natural surroundings.*

Above: *Rambling roses trained over a wooden archway make a charming entrance to a planted garden area.*

apertures

Solid barriers sometimes feel rather oppressive, but the introduction of carefully positioned gaps or "windows" can bring about a transformation, as well as offering opportunities for theatrical effects.

ABOVE: *Window-like apertures can be partially screened to baffle the eye. Stone balustrades are used here but you can also use decorative metal grilles or even coloured glass.*

LEFT: *A window in this avant-garde screen provides visual relief through contrast. Notice how, in keeping with the design, fragments of the wire overlap the rim.*

OPPOSITE: *Glass screens, including those made from glass bricks, are increasingly being used as subtle dividers in outdoor spaces. This narrow aperture offers a tantalizing glimpse of the garden.*

With care, circular or rectangular apertures, including long vertical slits too narrow to be used as doorways, can be cut into existing boundary hedges to reveal glimpses of the countryside beyond – grazing animals, distant hills, the sea. This is a technique sometimes seen in Japanese Zen gardens and modern minimalist settings, carefully orchestrating and adding significance to what the garden visitor sees and experiences. In a built-up area you might be able to create a sight-line through a wall to an attractive piece of architecture. The great advantage of apertures is that you can select the best elements of a view and frame them, while at the same time blocking out any undesirable features.

Providing a window or *clairvoyée* that looks into the garden from the outside – giving passers-by a pleasant surprise – or that creates a tantalizing vignette of a garden room can also be highly effective. Use the contrast of light and colour to full advantage when setting up these visual treats. For example, the excitement of spying an otherwise hidden garden can be greatly enhanced if you are standing in a relatively green, shady setting looking on to a brightly lit spot full of scarlet, orange and yellow blooms. Water is another eye-catching element, and a sparkling fountain or a turquoise blue pool would be sure to attract attention.

One of the oldest types of aperture is the Chinese moon gate, so called because of its circular profile. These may be large enough to step through but are not necessarily entranceways, being used more like frames through which to view a garden scene. Other Oriental cultures, and those with an Arabic influence, have also used apertures to great effect, fitting decorative grilles or screens that allow light to flood into the garden, sometimes creating attractive shadow patterns. Grilles and trelliswork baffle the eye, and although it is possible to see through them, the focus is kept within the garden.

Moderately priced off-the-peg materials are available, but with a little imagination it is possible to upgrade these basic building blocks to create stylish garden features.

When you start out with a blank canvas it is possible to take the boundary décor in a number of directions, depending on the materials and colours you use. A lacklustre wall or fence can be "rescued" with a lick of paint or decorative detailing, such as new coping stones. You might flood the walls with coloured light in the evening to provide instant atmosphere for entertaining, or create a Spanish-style courtyard by decorating the walls with colourful ceramic tiles or a sparkling water feature. Meanwhile, mismatched fence panels could be clad with heather screen-roll to make a uniform backdrop for a contemporary space. For a more traditional look, paint a fence in a dark colour and add a paler coloured trellis façade and acorn finials.

finishing effects

painted colour

The effect of paints and stains applied to walls, fences, trellis and metalwork is instant – painting is one of the simplest ways to transform the garden environment and create different moods and atmospheres.

There has never been a wider range of specialist products for colouring exterior wood, concrete, brickwork and metal; if you can't quite find the shade you are looking for, you can simply blend paints or stains or have them custom-mixed at your local store. Choosing the right colour can be tricky, and with wood treatments you will often find that the finished effect is rather different to that indicated on the container. This is partly due to the fact that absorption of the product is affected by the age and condition of the timber and any previous treatments it may have been given.

Gentle green, blue and lavender shades are easy to live with and make a pleasing backdrop for most border plantings. These are restful colours that make us feel calm and relaxed. In certain areas of the garden, such as a terrace used for entertaining and outdoor dining, it can be good to inject a note of vibrancy. Red and orange shades can imbue areas with energy and warmth and bring to mind desert or tropical locations. In climates where the dull days outnumber the sunny ones, the light spectrum is weighted towards blue, so you need to choose hot colours carefully lest they appear too harsh. Earthy or maroon reds, burnt sienna and terracotta are preferable to scarlet or clear orange, which are best restricted to minor detailing. Painting some adjacent elements in blue or green can also help to cool things down. For example, you might combine teal-coloured trelliswork with terracotta walls.

For the more adventurous among us, there are vivid pinks, purples and fizzy lime green - great fun for children and adults alike, but best used sparingly and preferably in private areas of the garden that are not overlooked – your neighbours may not share your taste. These colours work particularly well in contemporary settings, and combine beautifully with modern metal surfaces, such as chrome and polished stainless steel, as well as whitewashed or deep cornflower blue walls.

OPPOSITE: *This design relies on shape and texture for effect – the arc of fencing laths, the smooth curved seat, and the floor of stone shards. The greatest impact is created by its intense and surprising colour.*

TOP: *Painted in a shade of verdigris, the colour of this fence sets off the flowers and foliage.*

ABOVE: *Soft blues turn this picket fence into a pretty feature.*

White is often chosen to give a stylish, sophisticated and spacious feel to an area, as it is a colour that is associated with simplicity and minimalism. It is also a traditional choice for rural dwellings and cottages, and because of its heat-reflecting qualities it is widely used in hot climates to keep buildings cool. But in temperate regions with a higher rainfall, brilliant white can feel rather stark, and it can be hard to keep smart without frequent re-applications. White brightens gloomy areas, but for a softer alternative – in a shady courtyard, for example – try painting walls or an overlaying trellis façade in pale apple green, dove grey or even blush pink. If you already have a white rendered wall, you could tint it with another shade, such as lemon, simply by applying acrylic emulsion paint very roughly with a large pasting brush.

A more aged or distressed finish can help to engender a relaxed feel for your garden room, and though some shades, such as aubergine or magenta, look best when used to create a solid block of colour, natural shades reminiscent of water, earth or sky can benefit from a more diffuse look. On walls, gradually build up lighter or darker layers of colour over a base coat, using dilute washes until you achieve the right effect.

Preparing walls for painting with coloured masonry paint may simply be a case of brushing down the brickwork with a wire brush. Feature walls painted in a bold shade may be more effective if they are first rendered to give a smoother finish. It is a little like preparing a giant canvas. In fact a coloured wall can behave exactly like a piece of modern art.

Various effects can also be used to enhance the decorative value of trellis and fencing, including painting or staining the outer frame of a trellis panel, the wooden fencing posts and finials in a darker or lighter shade. For real drama go for a marked contrast, such as deep blue posts with light aquamarine infills. Painting fence panels by hand is slow work, especially when the wood is weathered, because the stain soaks in readily. Consider using a roller or hiring a sprayer.

RIGHT: *Sizzling hot, vibrant colour energizes this alfresco dining area. As well as painting the rendered wall, this contemporary design also utilizes wall plaques that boost the colour and act as pieces of abstract art.*

adding ornament

There are almost as many ways to embellish the "walls" of your garden room as can be used inside the house. As well as painting, you can hang pictures, apply wall coverings and even display ornaments.

Flat-topped walls with a staggered or stepped profile make an excellent staging for ornaments, as do apertures and niches. Pick objects that enhance the chosen theme of the garden. For example, in a plot reminiscent of a Tuscan villa you might place a classical bust or a terracotta vase in a niche, or top a wall pillar with a dramatic potted agave. In more contemporary surroundings, you could simply arrange some beautifully shaped beach pebbles or position coloured glass bottles in narrow gaps that let in the light.

Conjuring an air of faded elegance takes a little theatrical stage-setting. Try placing classical urns or statuary on plinths rising out of a romantic tangle of brambles and wild flowers. You could arrange broken sections of suitably aged stone balustrading along the boundary line, or build a folly in the form of a ruined wall. A more ambitious project could involve erecting a pair of antique ironwork gates, evoking a long-forgotten entranceway. For a more contemporary garden, add minimalist scupltured pieces to add interest in front of plain fencework, hedges or railings.

To decorate fencing and trellis, use machine-turned wooden finials, such as balls or acorns, to replace the existing flat-topped post caps. These can be picked out in a different colour to the rest of the woodwork to make them even more eye-catching. Wooden finials usually have a screw embedded in them – simply drill holes in the tops of the posts and screw them into position. A limited range of finials for topping brick and stone pillars is available from builders' merchants, but you can usually find more ornate designs, in carved stone or terracotta, at architectural salvage merchants.

LEFT: *Oversized terracotta pots and exotic agaves combine to give a distinctly Mediterranean look and make a strong decorative statement set at regular intervals, like finials, along this brick boundary wall.*

RIGHT: *The fine horizontal slats of this unusual wooden sculpture contrast well with the bold, vertical garden fence posts beyond.*

BELOW: *Classical stone statuary adds an impressive detail to this shady corner of the garden and creates a strong focal point that holds the collection of planted terracotta pots together.*

To add drama to a plain painted wall, try hanging a large contemporary wall plaque, such as a sun symbol, keeping the surroundings free of clutter so that it can be properly appreciated. Another modern treatment involves attaching sheets of highly reflective stainless steel. This is ideal for small urban plots because it has the effect of visually opening out the space. Place pots of large-leaved foliage plants in front for a really lush effect. Sheets of galvanized aluminium or zinc could be used instead if you prefer a matt effect. Mild steel has a more "organic" feel as it gradually develops beautifully coloured rust, and copper sheeting slowly weathers to produce blue-green verdigris.

Some decorations work best when they are set into the fabric of the wall, rather than being fixed on to the surface. For example, if you were rendering a wall you could incorporate a decorative stone-effect plaque, a wall-mounted sundial, some patterned tiles or a small mosaic panel into the cement. Camouflaging the edges of this kind of decoration, either with rendering or foliage, adds to the illusion that the object has perhaps been there for many years.

Using waterproof tile adhesive you can also create simple mosaics, using glass tesserae, broken pieces of coloured ceramic or mirror shards, seashells or small beach pebbles. Plan your design on paper first and, if possible, transfer the key dimensions and shapes to the wall before you begin working. It may be easier to apply the design to a weatherproof board that can be worked on indoors and fixed on to the wall on

OPPOSITE: Small pieces of glass tesserae have been used in a mosaic pattern to break up the monotony of the white rendered wall in this small courtyard setting. If you don't feel up to such a creative task, you could buy whole tiles and use them in an easy-to-apply geometric pattern.

ABOVE FROM LEFT: Stone slabs imprinted with alphabetical letters add a novelty feature to this brick wall. Glass fishing floats hanging in nets make a perfect decorative detail for the fencing of a seashore-themed wooden deck. Terracotta pots planted with bright geraniums add colour and vibrancy to a roughly rendered wall in this Mediterranean garden.

completion. Another simple but very effective idea is to use a rectangular piece of split slate, such as a roofing tile, as the backdrop to a mosaic design. This can then be hung on the garden wall in the same way as a picture indoors.

A rendered breezeblock (cinderblock) wall can look out of place in a country garden. To give the illusion of a wall built from stone or weathered brick, you might intersperse odd groupings of these more attractive materials and render around them to leave them half-exposed. Along similar lines, you could also set into the wall a stone corbel or plinth, or a shelf made from a flat-topped piece of rock. Jutting out from the vertical surface, this could then be used to display some kind of decorative element, such as a planted pot, an ornate lantern or a small piece of sculpture. The advantage here is that the ornament itself can be replaced whenever you like, perhaps to tie it in with the season or the theme of a social occasion.

decorative façades

Plain walls and fences can seem lacklustre, especially if you can't plant anything against them, but you can turn boundaries into garden features simply by applying a variety of decorative structures.

A simple way to revamp a plain wall is to attach trellis panels, which are now available in a wide range of attractive shapes and designs. If you are intending to grow plants up from the base, ensure you leave a gap behind the panels so that the plants can climb unimpeded. Do this by attaching the panels to wooden battens – roofing laths are ideal. A wooden framework could also support heather, willow or bamboo cladding attached with a staple gun.

Some styles of treillage include window-shaped apertures and you could use a mirrored surface to reflect the surrounding greenery and create the illusion of a window. False perspective panels are also very effective in formal courtyard situations, helping to make a small garden seem larger. Experiment by placing a piece of statuary or a flower-filled vase on a plinth in the foreground to add depth to the picture. An arch-shaped trellis panel could be used to frame a wall-mounted fountain. Contrasting coloured trellis with a paler or darker background can be particularly striking, and the addition of a few props in the right colour range also works wonders.

Use trellis and posts to build a false façade around a French window or patio doors, subtly emphasizing the garden entrance with airy latticework "columns" and overhead "beams". Construct a pergola to enliven a dull corner or create an arbour for permanent outdoor seating by attaching a sloping roof to a wall. For the look of an authentic Italian loggia, use stout posts of reclaimed timber and cover the roof with terracotta pantiles.

ABOVE LEFT: *The combination of glazed coping and lacquer red trellis turns this wall into an extravagant chinoiserie folly.*

LEFT: *Delicate treillage augments the entrance to this balcony garden with a Renaissance flavour echoed by the fountain and topiary.*

RIGHT: *This sheltered corner has been transformed into a secluded garden room by building a pergola out over the deck. Panels of trellis enclose the space without blocking out the light, and are painted in fresh white to complement the smart blue of the overhead beams.*

BELOW: *Construction blocks, with natural bricks inserted for contrast, are used in their natural state to create a cheap and imaginative façade for a plain-painted wall.*

lighting

As well as being functional, lighting can be highly decorative, and there are a number of techniques that can be employed to transform your boundaries at night and add a touch of theatre to the garden.

TOP: *Candles can be fixed to trellis to illuminate a patio or terrace.*

ABOVE: *This elegant antique-style wall lantern has a practical function as well as adding decorative detail.*

OPPOSITE: *Candles and oil lamps add a romantic ambience as they illuminate the path leading to a secluded corner of the garden. Mini spotlights or fairy lights would make a more practical option.*

When walls and screens are divided into regular segments, for example by brick piers or stout posts, the rhythm and regularity of the construction can be emphasized using mini floodlights angled to illuminate them from the base. Coloured light can make a really dramatic statement and change the mood of the space significantly, particularly with white or very pale rendered walls. Modern materials, such as glass brick walls, galvanized mesh screening or stainless steel cladding, come to life and can appear even more avant-garde when lit creatively. Even formal hedges can be lit to accentuate their crisp architectural lines, as can features such as alcoves, while the fluttering leaves of a planted screen of bamboo can be captured at night by mini uplighters.

You can use decorative lamps in place of finials to create a modern or period feel for a wall or entranceway, and there are scores of different designs for wall lights, ranging from hi-tech and contemporary to rustic and quirky. If you can't find what you are looking for in lighting shops and do-it-yourself stores, try mail-order companies via the internet. Some bulkhead lights are small enough to be screwed on to wooden fence posts, and traditional brass fittings would work well with sleeper walls at a beach-side residence. In an open-plan housing development you can mark boundary lines subtly by using simple, low-level lamps run off a transformer, or possibly solar-powered units that switch on automatically at dusk.

Well-lit water features give double the pleasure, and you can employ new technology, such as optical fibres, to light up cascades or fountain jets in a magical way. You might also put an uplighter in the reservoir below a wall mask, so that the features are dramatically illuminated.

Perforated walls or ones with a series of niches are ideal for candles, helping to create a romantic ambience. Use lanterns or glass nightlight covers to prevent the flames being blown out.

water features

Built into one of the boundary walls or internal divisions in the garden, it can be relatively simple to create a focal point that makes full use of the sight and sound of moving water.

Raised pools or reservoirs are popular schemes for wall settings: half-moon pool shapes can be made from bricks or rendered breezeblocks (cinderblocks), while rectangular or trough-like designs can be constructed from building blocks or wooden sleepers. For a contemporary finish, apply metal cladding or painted rendering. Line the pool with black butyl rubber or seal the internal surface of porous brickwork and concrete with bituminastic paint.

The reservoir can house a simple fountain spray, but more usually the water comes from a mask or spout mounted on the wall above. These decorative focal points come in many designs, from classical Greco-Roman or Mediterranean, such as lions' heads and pagan gods, to rustic, such as reproductions of antique hand pumps. Contemporary ideas range from utilitarian objects, such as taps and watering cans, to abstract sculptures in ceramic or stainless steel. A cascade or smooth curtain of water is another modern alternative, pouring over a flat shelf of metal, Perspex (Plexiglas) or slate. To achieve a really even flow, fit an attachment that feeds the water through a perforated bar. Cascades can also be made to flow down a curtain of chains directly into the reservoir below.

The speed of the water is governed by the flow regulator on the submersible pump, and this should be adjusted to achieve just the right sound and visual effect. Too fast a stream can sound hollow and unnatural, especially when the water is falling from quite a height. Sometimes problems with sound can be remedied by placing a few cobbles near the water surface to disperse the jet. Take care that the water isn't splashing out of the reservoir, as this will eventually drain the tank and cause the pump to burn out. You can buy self-contained wall-mounted water features that simply plug into a convenient electricity supply, but these need careful monitoring because their reservoirs are very small.

OPPOSITE: *A water curtain would enliven any plain wall, and such an arrangement would be ideal for a garden that slopes up steeply from the house, helping to soften the retaining walls or terracing that are prominent features in the view.*

ABOVE: *The grotto-like effect of this wall mask and pool is enhanced by the lush planting surrounding it. The pipework feeding into the mask from the pool pump below is hidden from view on the other side of the wall.*

TOP: *A simple pebble pool and fountain makes an interesting focal point in this boundary corner.*

ABOVE: *A wall fountain with a tiny electric pump is easy to install.*

OPPOSITE: *Raised wall pools are perfect for creating the effect of a cool oasis in a paved courtyard, but you must ensure that they are perfectly sealed to prevent moisture seeping out into the wall behind.*

To create the feel of a Moorish or Spanish courtyard, you could use tiles to clad the wall behind the water feature, as well as the reservoir itself. Use exterior-quality waterproof tile adhesive. Frostproof tiles in plain, deep blue would work well, as would terracotta with some patterned inserts or borders. Consider making the wall of the reservoir wide enough to double as impromptu seating, so that you can dabble your fingers in the water. A feature such as this would be ideal at the end of a walkway under a shady pergola.

If young children use the garden a water feature needs to be safe – the reservoir needs to be either covered or concealed below ground level. Wall fountains with hidden reservoirs can have a contemporary feel, especially when the area surrounding the cascade is very open and simply decorated. A plastic cold-water storage tank sunk into the ground would make an ideal container. You could extend the water catchment area by overlapping the rim with a butyl rubber pond liner, set at a shallow angle to direct the flow back into the main tank. Cover the tank with a rigid metal grille and camouflage it with pebbles and cobbles.

For a more naturalistic effect, you can run a trickle of water down the face of a rugged stone or slate wall or an insert made from these materials. Algae will soon colonize the glistening rock and you can strengthen the illusion by planting ferns and other foliage plants in the surrounding crevices. Take care to seal the watercourse as water can find its way through the smallest of gaps, and with hidden leaks it can be difficult to maintain levels in the reservoir. A safer option to create a grotto effect on a shady wall would be to set a mask into the stonework, so that the water is directed into the reservoir.

Stylish screens, made from coloured Perspex (Plexiglas) sheets, opaque safety glass panels or glass bricks, let in light and are ideal for sheltering sitting areas and spaces used for outdoor dining and entertaining in contemporary settings. In combination with lush foliage plants, this kind of structure can be turned into a cooling water feature simply by running water down the face of the screen into a hidden reservoir below. Fix a perforated tube along the top of the screen so that the water trickles out evenly down the face.

trompe l'oeil

For tiny backyard plots it is well worth employing some kind of visual trickery to create the illusion that the garden extends far beyond the boundary lines. Even simple techniques can be highly effective.

False perspective panels can cleverly fool the eye, to give the impression of archways or tunnels leading out of the garden. These specialist panels are made from treillage or cut from marine-quality ply. They work best fitted to a plain-painted or smooth-rendered wall. Complete the illusion by adding a weatherproof mirror cut to fit the door-like opening. Placing a statue or vase on a pedestal just in front of the "doorway" will add depth and perspective.

Large mirrors can also be fixed behind arched trellis panels or wrought iron gates. Reflecting the greenery from the rest of the garden, they make you feel as if you are looking through to another area. Again, the illusion can be strengthened by placing a large decorative element in front and also by camouflaging the edges of the aperture with foliage. A similar effect can be achieved by positioning a circular or arched window frame with a mirror behind it. A more avant-garde approach is to cover the wall, or sections of it, with mirror tiles to create intriguing multi-faceted reflections.

Murals employing false perspectives are a charming way of expanding the garden boundaries, as well as creating a make-believe view. Try to link features painted in the mural with real structures and objects set in the foreground, such as stone balustrading or identically planted containers.

If you are just starting to grow climbers up trellis panels on a plain wall, and the plants are only very small, you can multiply the apparent foliage cover simply by using leaf stencils or leaf-shaped stamps. Overlap the shapes and vary the shading between light and dark to capture the effect of natural light and shadow. Where the boundary is camouflaged by dense planting, you have the perfect opportunity to utilize another trick: laying a pathway or simply a curving line of stepping-stones that disappears into the shrubbery gives the illusion that the garden extends much further than it really does.

ABOVE: *This impressive trompe l'oeil mural, painted on to a previously featureless wall, not only decorates the garden and gives it a classical theme, but also makes it feel much bigger.*

OPPOSITE: *Though the boundary is just around this hidden corner, the impression is that the garden extends much further. Anyone exploring the pathway could be rewarded with some kind of decorative element.*

planting

You can create a veritable "hanging gardens" effect with overflowing troughs, baskets and wall planters. Where space is limited, walls and fences offer plenty of extra planting opportunities.

ABOVE: *Weighty timber planters have been stocked with a selection of hardy evergreens that give wind-protection to delicate flowering plants on this urban roof terrace. The planters have been attached to the terrace railings with metal clips to prevent movement in the wind.*

OPPOSITE: *A combination of rosemary, rambling honeysuckle and ivy covers this high brick-built garden wall, adding old-fashioned elegance and a beautiful scent that will fill the whole garden area at the end of a summer's day.*

Sheer boundary walls are easily softened using climbers and wall shrubs, so that verdant foliage and flowers trail down from above, as well as growing upwards. Cascading plants can disguise less-than-perfect fence panels and walls, and in new gardens you can create instant lushness with containers filled with summer annuals and tender perennials. Fast-growing trailers include *Bidens ferulifolia*; *Scaevola aemula* 'Blue Wonder'; Surfinia petunias; Tapien and Temari verbenas; ivies; *Glechoma hederacea* 'Variegata'; continental or cascade geraniums (*Pelargonium*) and *Helichrysum petiolare*.

Brackets can be fixed at the tops of fence posts, helping to create a visual rhythm once the baskets are in place, and you can also hang baskets at different heights to cover a large area. Metal potholders or clips allow you to mount an array of individual clay or plastic pots on a wall. By filling these with vibrant geraniums you could create a Mediterranean-style display on a sunny, whitewashed wall.

Attaching simple, straight-sided rectangular planting troughs to the top of a wall, or arranging them in staggered formation on the face, can create a more contemporary look than traditional hanging baskets, especially if all the containers are painted the same colour as the backdrop. For urban chic, try fixing galvanized metal planters to a rendered wall and planting them with stylish foliage varieties, including a mix of hardy evergreens and ground cover plants, such as ornamental grasses and sedges, *Campanula poscharskyana* 'Stella', clipped box balls and plain green ivy.

Fragrance adds another dimension, and many container plants have a delightful scent that sometimes lingers long after sundown, when heat continues to radiate from warm walls. For perfume at nose level, fill baskets with petunias; violas and pansies; verbenas; sweet white alyssum; *Brachyscome multifida*, bidens and herbs such as thyme, marjoram, mint and sage.

Camouflaging the true extent of boundaries with a luxuriant covering of foliage and flower can help to make a small garden feel much larger. Tender plants also really benefit from the microclimate generated by a warm, sunny wall or fence.

In a sheltered spot you could try exotic-looking wall shrubs such as fremontodendron, ceanothus, bottle brush (*Callistemon*), abutilon and *Magnolia grandiflora*. If you are choosing climbers for a warm position, you might include such gems as passionflower, trumpet vine, *Trachelospermum jasminoides* and *Clematis armandii*.

In cooler conditions, consider combining shade-tolerant wall shrubs, such as camellias, *Fatsia japonica*, *Viburnum tinus*, *Rhamnus alaternus* 'Argenteovariegata' and *Choisya* 'Aztec Pearl', with climbers such as *Rosa* 'The New Dawn'; honeysuckles; large-flowered white clematis and *Hedera colchica* 'Dentata Variegata'. This combination of glossy architectural leaves, variegation and pale flowers would really add sparkle.

The best and least conspicuous way to provide support for climbers and walls shrubs, including roses, is to attach horizontal lines of galvanized training wire at 45cm (18in) intervals up the wall. For climbers such as clematis, jasmine and honeysuckle, twist vertical supports round the horizontals to create a series of large squares. To keep the wire clear of the wall or fence so that air can circulate behind the plants, thread it through vine eyes, which either tap into mortar or screw into brick, concrete or wooden fence posts. Attach the stems to the outside of the support framework, as this allows for easier pruning and maintenance. Use soft twine, not wire or plastic, which can cut into the stems.

Some wall shrubs, such as camellias, may not need tying into the wall as such, but should be pruned to remove shoots growing straight out from the support to keep a more pleasing profile. Self-clinging climbers, including ivies and the climbing hydrangea (*Hydrangea anomala* subsp. *petiolaris*) may need help at first to get them to cling. Try using nail-on plastic ties to hold the stems in position. Both can take a couple of years to grow in earnest. Plant climbers and wall shrubs at least 45cm (18in) away from the wall or fence, to avoid concrete footings and keep the roots out of the rain shadow at its foot.

TOP: *Large-flowered clematis hybrids make a stunning show. White forms are especially effective on shady walls, along with green and white ivy.*

ABOVE: *Climbing roses can be grown up wooden trellis panels. Train branches horizontally for better flowering and fix with soft twine.*

OPPOSITE: *Clematis 'Montana' grows quickly and can easily smother large brick walls and fences, so take care where you plant it and keep it well away from other climbers. Some cultivars, such as 'Elizabeth', have a delightful sweet perfume.*